STEM IN THE STANLEY CUP

BY KRISTY STARK, M.A.ED.

CONTENT CONSULTANT

JESSE WILCOX, PHD

ASSISTANT PROFESSOR OF STEM EDUCATION

SIMPSON COLLEGE

SportsZone

An Imprint of Abdo Publishing

abdobooks.com

ABDOBOOKS.COM

Published by Abdo Publishing, a division of ABDO, PO Box 398166, Minneapolis, Minnesota 55439.

Printed in the United States of America, North Mankato, Minnesota
102019
012020

THIS BOOK CONTAINS RECYCLED MATERIALS

Cover Photo: Michael Tureski/Icon Sportswire/AP Images
Interior Photos: Roy K. Miller/Icon Sportswire/AP Images, 4–5, 8–9, 45; Chris Williams/Icon Sportswire/AP Images, 7; Frank Gunn/The Canadian Press/AP Images, 11; Jeff Roberson/AP Images, 12, 42; Kostas Lymperopoulos/Cal Sport Media/AP Images, 15, 20–21; Red Line Editorial, 16; Aaron Doster/Cal Sport Media/AP Images, 19; Darren Calabrese/The Canadian Press/AP Images, 23; Fred Kfoury III/Icon Sportswire/AP Images, 24; George Retseck Illustrations © Zamboni Company, 27; Mark J. Terrill/AP Images, 28–29; Marcio Jose Sanchez/AP Images, 31; George Silk/The LIFE Picture Collection/Getty Images, 32; AP Images, 34 (top); Michael Dwyer/AP Images, 34 (bottom); John McCreary/Icon Sportswire/AP Images, 37; Ric Tapia/Icon Sportswire/AP Images, 38–39; Bardocz Peter/Shutterstock Images, 41

Editor: Marie Pearson
Series Designer: Dan Peluso

LIBRARY OF CONGRESS CONTROL NUMBER: 2019941987

PUBLISHER'S CATALOGING-IN-PUBLICATION DATA
Names: Stark, Kristy, author.
Title: STEM in the Stanley Cup / by Kristy Stark
Description: Minneapolis, Minnesota : Abdo Publishing, 2020 | Series: STEM in the greatest sports events | Includes online resources and index.
Identifiers: ISBN 9781532190568 (lib. bdg.) | ISBN 9781644943144 (pbk.) | ISBN 9781532176418 (ebook)
Subjects: LCSH: Stanley Cup (Hockey)--Juvenile literature. | Sports sciences--Juvenile literature. | Applied science--Juvenile literature. | Ice hockey--Juvenile literature. | Physics--Juvenile literature.
Classification: DDC 796.015--dc23

TABLE OF CONTENTS

Nicklas Backstrom of the Washington Capitals passes the puck during the Stanley Cup playoffs.

CHAPTER 1

THE ROAD TO THE STANLEY CUP

It's Game 5 of the 2018 Stanley Cup Final. The Washington Capitals are battling the Las Vegas Golden Knights. Washington leads the series 3–1. During the second period, the Capitals' John Carlson has the puck at the center line. Carlson passes it across the ice to Nicklas Backstrom. Backstrom angles a pass to Alexander Ovechkin on the left side of the goal. Ovechkin quickly slaps the puck into the left corner of the goal. He scores! The Capitals go on to win the game and with it, the Stanley Cup.

STEM ON ICE

Every October the National Hockey League (NHL) starts a new season. Each team plays 82 games in the regular season. At the start of the season, there are 31 teams. Sixteen of them will reach the playoffs. The teams hope to make it to the playoffs. They want to win the Stanley Cup. It is hockey's highest honor and prize. Only one team wins the right to be called champions. In 2018 that team was the Capitals.

Hockey is a rough, high-speed game. Players need to skate well and not be afraid to make contact with other players. Physical skill is important. But so are science, technology, engineering, and math (STEM) concepts. Science explains how the puck moves across the ice. Technology helps fans follow the game and helps officials get the calls right. Engineering helps keep players safe while letting them move quickly across

Alexander Ovechkin celebrates a goal during Game 5 of the 2018 Stanley Cup Final.

the ice. Math shows how players can make effective passes off the boards, and it also supplies fans with many fun statistics about the game. STEM concepts make the Stanley Cup even more exciting to enjoy each year.

Science explains how objects move across the ice.

CHAPTER 2

THE SCIENCE OF HOCKEY

While playing hockey, players may not actively think about science. But science plays a role in all aspects of the game, including motion.

Sir Isaac Newton was a scientist who worked in the 1600s. He studied math and science. He is well known for three laws that describe how objects move in the world around us. These ideas apply to items on the ice of a hockey rink.

Newton's first law states that an object at rest will stay at rest until some force makes it move. The law also says that a moving object will continue to move until something stops it. This is called inertia. A hockey player can stand still on the ice. He will continue to stand still until a force causes him to move. This force could come from his own muscles pushing him forward. Or it could come from a player from the other team. Players often collide and bodycheck each other during games. One player's body hitting another player is a powerful force. Both players experience a change in motion. The force causes a change in their speed and direction.

Players work hard to score goals. They move and pass the puck all over the ice. Their sticks strike the puck with a lot force. That sends the puck down the ice

INJURIES

The force of colliding players often leads to injuries, including concussions. A concussion is an injury to the brain. When a force hits the head, it can cause the brain to quickly move and bounce around within the skull. This can damage the brain.

When one player checks another, both players experience a force pushing them away from the point of impact.

to teammates. This is related to Newton's second law. The second law states that the force acting on an object is equal to the mass of that object times its acceleration.

Many forces are at work when a player slams another player into the boards.

An NHL hockey puck is much easier to move on the ice than a heavier object, such as a bowling ball. An NHL hockey puck has a mass of 6 ounces (170 g). A bowling ball has a mass of 10 pounds (4.5 kg) or more. It would take more force to move a bowling ball than a puck. Since a puck has a light mass, players can make the puck travel more than 100 miles per hour (160 km/h). Because of this law of motion, all NHL hockey pucks must be exactly the same mass. If teams used pucks of various masses, it would change the amount of force needed to move the puck down the ice. It could give the team that is used to a particular puck an advantage over a team that uses a puck with a different mass.

Newton's third law states that every action has an opposite and equal reaction. When force is used on two objects, it has an equal effect on both objects. During games, players often collide with the boards around the rink. The force of a player hitting the boards has an effect on the board. It has an effect on the player, too. The force of a player hitting the board causes the plexiglass to move. The force of hitting the boards also causes the player to stop or even get thrown backward. The amount of force on both objects is the same.

PREPARING THE ICE

The road to the Stanley Cup involves other science, too. The ice is the most important thing in the game. Without ice, no one could play hockey.

The concept of making an ice rink is the same science behind making ice cubes. But it takes a more complex system to make an ice rink. Water freezes at 32 degrees Fahrenheit (0°C). But NHL teams play inside huge arenas, not small freezers. There are special pipes and coils under the floors. They are part of a cooling system that helps keep the ice frozen. The system has insulation that keeps the cold air in and warm air out.

It takes a whole crew to make the ice for a hockey rink. The crew works to make the rink about 1 inch (2.5 cm) thick. That inch is made up of lots of layers. The first layer is made with a fine mist of water. This layer is

It takes careful preparation to form the ice for a Stanley Cup rink.

LAYERS OF ICE

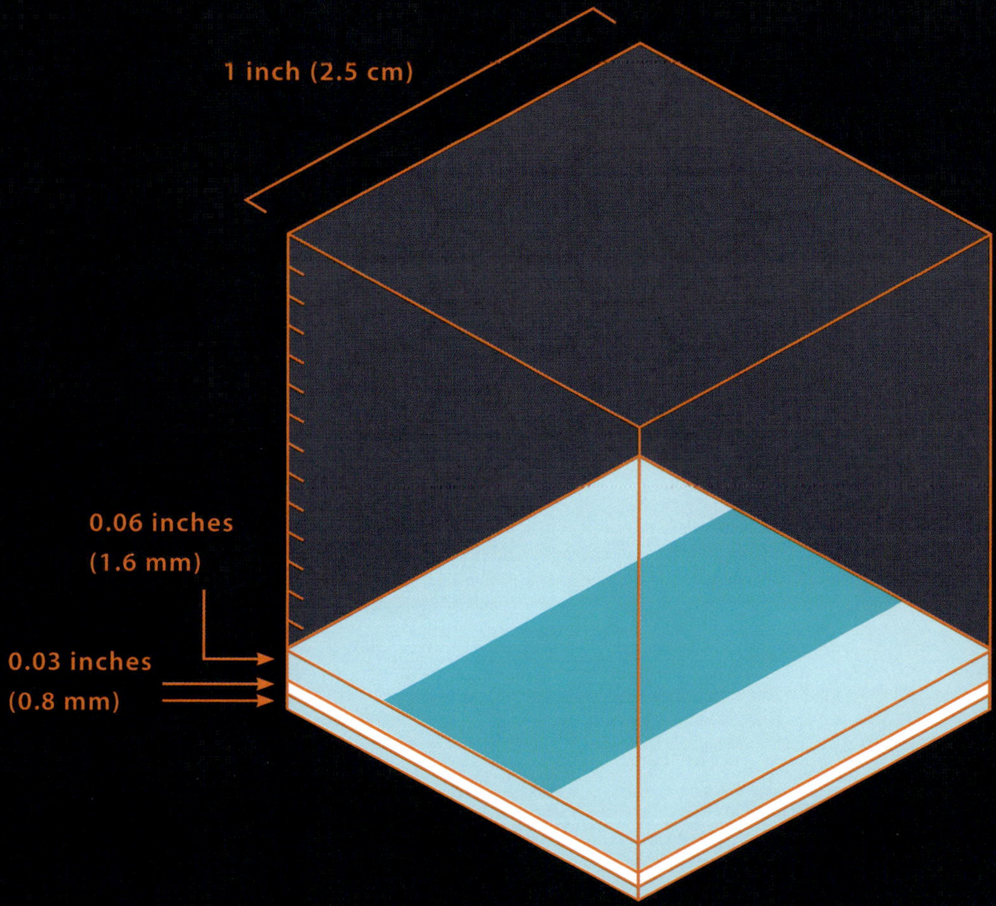

The ice on an NHL rink is put down in layers. Ice is a form of water. Matter has three typical forms. These forms are solid, liquid, and gas. Water is a liquid. Ice is its solid form. Temperature plays a big role in what form matter takes. Pure water becomes a solid (ice) at 32 degrees Fahrenheit (0°C). Pure water boils at 212 degrees Fahrenheit (100°C). A rink needs to be kept cooler than 32 degrees Fahrenheit (0°C) to make sure the ice stays frozen.

approximately 0.03 inches (0.8 mm) thick. The crew waits for the cooling system to freeze the layer. Then they add another layer. It is as thick as the first one. When that layer is frozen, workers paint the ice white. The white background helps players and fans see the black puck on the ice. Another layer of mist is added on top of the white paint. This layer is approximately 0.06 inches (1.6 mm) thick. Then workers paint the colored lines of the rink and add the team logo at center ice.

After the paint dries, the crew adds the final layers of water. Between each of the many layers, they must allow the ice to freeze. It takes 15 to 20 hours just to make these final layers of ice. It takes about 12,000 to 15,000 gallons (45,000–57,000 L) of water to make a hockey rink. Of that, 10,000 gallons (38,000 L) are used for the final layers. After the long process of making the ice, the surface of the ice has to stay at approximately 24 degrees Fahrenheit (minus-4.4°C). The system under the floor helps maintain this temperature. It ensures that the surface stays frozen. The temperature inside the arena is also kept cool. The air needs to be kept between 50 and 60 degrees Fahrenheit (10–16°C) to help maintain ideal ice conditions. Some hockey fans need to bundle up to watch a Stanley Cup game in person.

Ice conditions may determine the outcome of a game. In the 2019 Stanley Cup playoffs, the Boston Bruins played the Toronto Maple Leafs. Throughout the series, the ice conditions at Boston's TD Garden were not ideal. Hot and humid weather conditions kept the ice's surface from being solid and smooth. Boston's Brad Marchand said the ice was horrible. He thought the ice was why the series was tied after Game 6. However, Boston won Game 7 to win the series.

Ice resurfacing machines make the ice smooth to help players and the puck glide across it.

Video boards help fans keep track of the score and see the action up close.

CHAPTER 3

TECH TIME

Technology helps teams play and win in the Stanley Cup. Companies make new devices for the hockey rink. Technology helps the players and referees during the Stanley Cup. Some video systems help fans to not miss any of the action on the ice. A special machine keeps the ice conditions perfect for the players.

TRACKING THE ACTION

Hockey is a high-speed game with lots of action. The players skate around the rink very quickly. It can be easy to miss a play.

Referees might miss something important. They might make a wrong call. It's especially important to avoid bad calls in Stanley Cup games. To keep things fair, the NHL reviews and confirms each goal. A video review room at NHL headquarters in Toronto is full of large televisions and computer screens. The screens get video feeds from all the cameras in the arena. There are wide-angle cameras above the rink. There are referee cameras that are close to the goals. All of the cameras capture the action on the ice. The cameras send the images to the video review team.

The official call by the video review team can decide the outcome of a game. This was the case in Game 2 of the 2008 Stanley Cup playoff series between the Washington Capitals and the Pittsburgh Penguins. In the third period, the Capitals led the game 3–1. The Penguins' Patric Hornqvist slapped the puck across the goal line. The Penguins thought they had cut Washington's lead in half. But the referee said that Hornqvist did not score a goal. He said that the puck

In the video review room, officials can view a play from multiple angles to determine the correct call.

did not fully cross the line. The call was replayed in the video review room. The review team watched the play many times. The review confirmed the referee's call, and the goal did not count. The no-goal call may have taken

Cameras are placed around the rink, including in the nets, so that officials in the video review room can get the best views on a play.

away some of the Penguins' momentum. They lost the game 4–1 and went on to lose the series to the Capitals.

TRACKING DATA

Each NHL team has a group of people who keep track of the players' statistics, or stats. They keep stats for every turnover, penalty, hit, shot, goal, and more. The stats teams use a system of computers and special software to keep track of each stat. They use the Hockey Information and Tracking System (HITS). All of the data is entered into HITS at once. It gives sports reporters and fans updated stats on their computers or smartphones. People on the other side of the world can see the

NEW SENSORS

In 2019 the NHL started using a new tracking system in all 31 of its arenas. The system uses sensors found inside the puck and on players. The sensors send signals that show the path of the puck on video. They also can give information about the speed of each player and the distance between players on the ice.

updated stats. No one misses out on the outcome of the game or data about their favorite player.

The stats teams use video replay to confirm data as needed. If data was recorded incorrectly, they can quickly update the stat in the system.

IDEAL ICE CONDITIONS

Keeping the ice in good shape is key to a great game. An ice resurfacing machine is the best way to keep the ice in top form. During the game, players' skates and sticks make the ice rough. The ice needs some work between periods to make it smooth again.

All 31 NHL rinks use ice resurfacing machines to resurface the ice. The machine scrapes off the rough top layer of ice and lays down a new, smooth layer. This ensures that the puck travels smoothly around the rink. The machine is a fan favorite too. Fans cheer for the resurfacing machine when it takes the ice.

Shaving

A blade (1) shaves a thin layer from the surface of the ice.

Collecting

After a horizontal screw (2) (auger) gathers the shavings, a vertical screw (3) propels them into the snow tank (4).

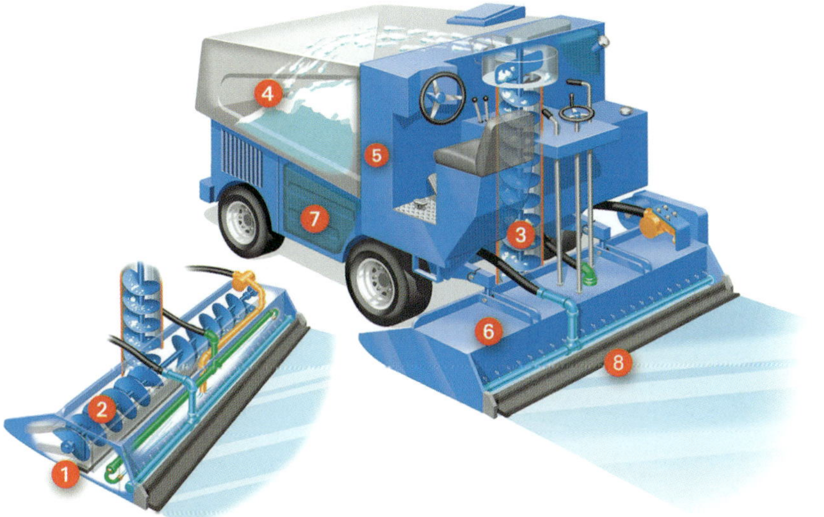

Washing

Water is fed from a wash-water tank (5) to the "conditioner" (6), which rinses the ice. Dirty water collected in front of a squeegee is vacuumed, filtered, and returned to the tank.

Resurfacing

Clean water from the ice making tank (7) is delivered to the ice through a pipe and spread evenly by a towel pulled across the ice behind the conditioner (8).

The Zamboni® ice resurfacing machine has a sharp blade that scrapes off a thin layer of ice. This gets rid of the grooves made by skates. The machine's operator drives in an oval pattern. The driver goes slowly to avoid making more nicks in the ice. The machine washes the ice surface with water and then vacuums up the dirty water. Finally, it sprays clean water back onto the ice. The water freezes into a smooth layer of ice. The ice is ready for the next period.

*ZAMBONI and the configuration of the Zamboni® ice resurfacing machine are registered in the U.S. Patent and Trademark Office as the trademarks of Frank J. Zamboni & Co., Inc.

Each part of a goalie's gear is carefully engineered.

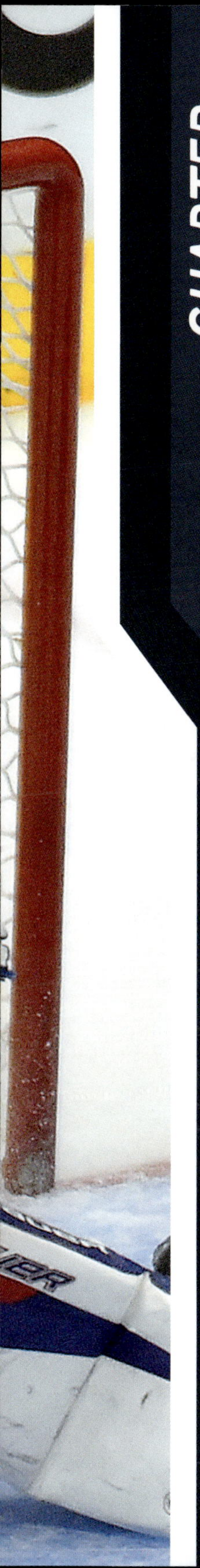

CHAPTER 4

ENGINEERED FOR SAFETY AND PERFORMANCE

Stanley Cup games rely on engineering concepts. Over the years, players and coaches have learned ways to make players safer and more effective on the ice. Protective equipment for goalies continues to improve. Engineers have even found ways to make hockey sticks perform better for players.

BODY PROTECTION

Players need to be protected from the puck, sticks, and other players. The goalie needs the most protection. The puck can move at more than 100 miles per hour (160 km/h). It flies straight at the goalie. So goalies wear lots of equipment. They wear thick leg pads. The pads are filled with foam. The foam provides a lot of cushion when they land on the ice to block a goal attempt. The pads also help the goalie keep an opponent from scoring. They can lie flat on the ice when the goalie is in a kneeling position. The puck may bounce off the legs while the pads protect the player.

Goalies are also decked out with special gloves and upper-body pads. The catching glove is similar to a catcher's mitt in baseball. The blocker is a glove with a wide, flat surface that covers the goalie's stick hand. These special gloves protect the goalie and help keep the puck out of the net. The pads are worn under the goalie's jersey. The pads protect the goalie's upper body.

A goalie's leg pads offer both protection and a barrier between the puck and goal.

This gear is constantly redesigned not only for protection, but also for speed and movement. In the past, the pads were filled with heavy foam. This made it hard for goalies to move. Now, the pads are filled with foam that is engineered to be lightweight yet still able to protect goalies from injury.

HEAD AND FACE PROTECTION

All hockey players wear helmets to stay safe. Goalies wear special masks that give added protection in the net. The masks have changed a lot in appearance since the sport's early days.

Jacques Plante models an early version of the fiberglass goalie's mask that he designed.

When the NHL started in 1917, goalies did not even wear masks or helmets. Clint Benedict of the Montreal Maroons was the first to wear a leather mask in 1930. But he did not wear it for long. The mask made it hard for him to see.

In 1959 the Montreal Canadiens goalie Jacques Plante was hit in the face with a puck. After that he designed his own mask. It was made from fiberglass. At first rival fans and coaches laughed at his mask. But after Plante's team won the Stanley Cup for the fifth year in a row in 1960, Plante's mask became popular. Many goalies started to wear similar masks.

During the 1980s, cage masks became more popular. The design made it easy for goalies to see. Modern goalie helmets have a built-in cage mask. The helmets are made from fiberglass. This material is lightweight. It is also sturdy and strong. It absorbs the impact of a puck, stick, or player that hits it. The front of the helmets still have a cage design. It keeps the puck from hitting a

In 1959 Jacques Plante (top) wore the very first goalie mask. He had made it himself out of fiberglass. The last year a goalie went onto the ice without a mask was 1974. Today's masks have steel bars around the eye area instead of small holes. This makes it easier for the goalie to see. They protect the throat in addition to the face. And today, many goalies decorate their masks with unique designs.

goalie's face. Many goalies have personalized designs on their helmets.

HISTORY OF HOCKEY STICKS

Hockey sticks also have changed a lot over time. They have been engineered to help players perform better. Sticks were once made of wood. Over the years, different types of wood were used to make stronger sticks. Designers used wood that was strong enough to handle a powerful shot without breaking. In the 1920s, ash wood was the material used to make most sticks because it is durable. The sticks were made from two separate pieces of wood. One piece made the shaft of the stick. The other piece made the blade. The blade was flat. The curved blades used today became commonly used in the 1960s. Curved blades give players better control of the puck.

Wooden sticks were heavy. They slowed players and their shots. Engineers looked for ways to make the sticks lighter. They wanted players to have sticks

CUSTOM STICKS

Some players work like engineers to customize their sticks. Wayne Gretzky is one of the greatest hockey players of all time. He used tape to make the stick's shaft more rounded. It gave him a better grip. Gretzky's engineering efforts, along with careful preparation, paid off. He won four Stanley Cup Finals during his career.

that were easier to handle. Over several decades, companies started to make sticks that used aluminum and fiberglass. These materials are much lighter than wood. In 1981 the NHL started to let players use aluminum sticks.

Today, the cores of most sticks are made of ash wood. Then the wood is wrapped in a blend of materials such as fiberglass, graphite, and aluminum. These materials add strength. They also keep the stick flexible and lightweight.

Hockey sticks need to be able to bend without breaking, such as during a slapshot.

Angles are a big part of hockey.

CHAPTER 5

MATH ALL AROUND

During the 2018 Stanley Cup Final, Alexander Ovechkin of the Washington Capitals was likely not thinking about math equations. But he was definitely aware of how to use angles to get the puck into the goal. He scored 15 goals during the playoffs. He used angles to pass the puck to teammates. He had 12 assists in playoff games. There is a lot of math in hockey, from the use of angles to measuring the top prize, the Stanley Cup trophy.

ANGLES OFF THE BOARDS

Players understand how to use angles to get the puck to where they want it to go. The boards around the ice help them angle shots. They can angle shots around opposing players. Or they can angle shots to pass the puck to a teammate. Using the boards is like having another teammate on the ice.

When the puck hits the boards, it bounces off at an equal angle. If the puck is shot against the boards at a 45-degree angle, it will come off the board at a 45-degree angle. Players use what they know about angles to chip the puck at the boards. They may do this to pass to a teammate while an opponent skates between them. On April 4, 2019, the Philadelphia Flyers were playing the St. Louis Blues in a Stanley Cup playoffs game. Scott Laughton of the Flyers expertly used the boards to get the puck past opposing players. The angle helped him get the puck to his teammate

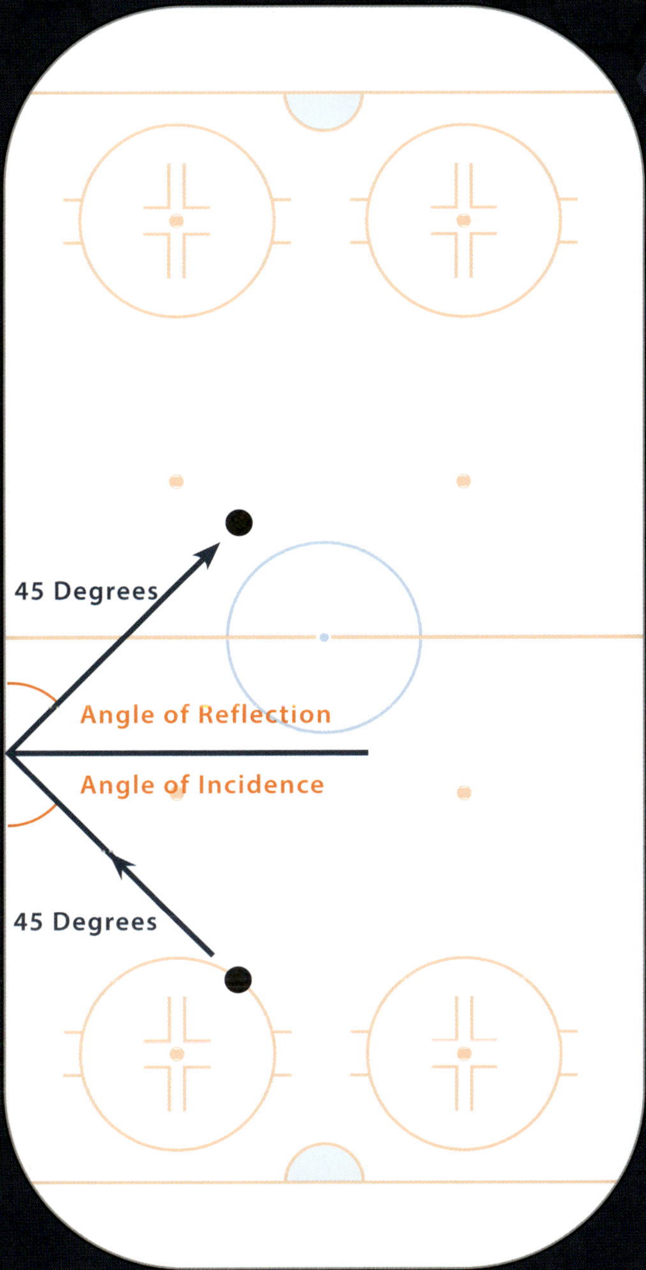

The angle at which the puck hits the boards is called the angle of incidence. When it bounces off the boards, it travels at the same angle. This is called the angle of reflection. A smart hockey player knows how to control this angle to get the puck exactly where he wants it.

The more straight-on a shot is, the wider an area the puck has to make it into the goal.

Oskar Lindblom. Lindblom got the puck from the angled pass and scored the Flyers' first goal of the game.

ANGLES AROUND THE NET

Hockey players must use angles to get the puck into the net. Goalies do their best to block most of the space near the goal. They rarely let players have an open, straight shot at the goal. Defenders help protect the goal, too. They work with the goalie to limit the angle of access to the goal. An opponent directly in front of the net has the most access to the goal because of the space on both sides of the goalie. But defenders can force the opponent to move to either side of the goal. This makes a smaller angle of access to the goal. It makes the shooter have to take a shot with a very small angle. There is less chance of the puck going into the net.

STANLEY CUP WINNERS

The Montreal Canadiens have won the Stanley Cup more times than any other team in the NHL. They have won 24 times through 2019. The Canadiens have won almost twice as many times as the Toronto Maple Leafs, the next closest team. Toronto has 13 wins.

THE STANLEY CUP

Players work hard all season to win the Stanley Cup trophy. The trophy was originally just the bowl on top. It is 7.3 inches (18.5 cm) tall and 11.4 inches (29 cm) across.

The bowl stays the same from year to year. But the base of the trophy changes over time. The players who win the Stanley Cup Final have their names engraved on the bands that make up the base. When a band is full, the oldest band is taken off. This keeps the trophy from getting too tall and too heavy to carry. With the bands, the trophy is 35.2 inches (89.5 cm) tall and weighs 34.2 pounds (15.5 kg).

Each player on the championship team gets the trophy for one day over the summer. Players have filled the bowl with lots of things. It has a volume of about 497 cubic inches (8,144 cubic cm), so it can hold a lot. The bowl can hold 14 12-ounce cans of soda. Players have been known to eat their morning cereal or a spaghetti dinner from the bowl.

Understanding STEM concepts can make Stanley Cup games all the more exciting.

The Stanley Cup playoffs are an exciting part of hockey. STEM concepts are involved in every aspect of the games. The more people know about STEM, the more exciting the games can be.

GLOSSARY

acceleration
An increase of speed in a certain direction.

force
An action that influences the motion of an object.

inertia
The property of physical things that says that an object that is not moving stays still, and an object that is moving goes at the same speed and in the same direction until a force affects it.

insulation
A material that is used to stop heat or cold from escaping an area.

mass
A measure of how much matter is in an object.

momentum
A combination of speed in a certain direction and mass.

playoffs
A series of games played after the end of the regular season and leading up to a championship game.

plexiglass
A clear plastic.

statistics
A set of numbers used to describe aspects of a game, such as scoring or rebounding numbers.

turnover
When the team loses the puck to the other team because of an error in play or penalty.

volume
The amount of space that is filled by something.

MORE INFORMATION

BOOKS

Graves, Will. *Ultimate NHL Road Trip*. Minneapolis, MN: Abdo Publishing, 2019.

Martin, Brett S. *STEM in Hockey*. Minneapolis, MN: Abdo Publishing, 2018.

Page, Sam. *Hockey: Then to Wow!* New York: Liberty Street, 2017.

ONLINE RESOURCES

Booklinks
NONFICTION NETWORK
FREE! ONLINE NONFICTION RESOURCES

To learn more about STEM in the Stanley Cup, visit **abdobooklinks.com** or scan this QR code. These links are routinely monitored and updated to provide the most current information available.

Kristy Stark writes books about a variety of topics, from the history of telephones to the game of Quidditch. When she is not busy writing, she enjoys running, reading, and doing just about anything outdoors. Most of all, she loves to spend time with her husband and two young children. They love to go swimming, hiking, or camping in the warm California sun.